WITHDRAWN

Jacqueline Kennedy

Jennifer Strand

abdopublishing.com

Published by Abdo Zoom™, PO Box 398166, Minneapolis, Minnesota 55439. Copyright © 2018 by Abdo Consulting Group, Inc. International copyrights reserved in all countries. No part of this book may be reproduced in any form without written permission from the publisher. Abdo Zoom™ is a trademark and logo of Abdo Consulting Group, Inc.

Printed in the United States of America, North Mankato, Minnesota
052017
092017

Cover Photo: Bettmann/Getty Images
Interior Photos: Bettmann/Getty Images, 1; Mark Shaw/Library of Congress, 4; AP Images, 5, 7, 9, 13, 16; Seth Poppel/Yearbook Library, 6; Toni Frissell/Library of Congress, 8; Sipa/AP Images, 10–11; Henry Burroughs/AP Images, 12; iStockphoto, 14; Cecil Stoughton/White House Photographs/John F. Kennedy Presidential Library and Museum/Boston, 15; Shutterstock Images, 17; Susan Ragan/AP Images, 18

Editor: Emily Temple
Series Designer: Madeline Berger
Art Direction: Dorothy Toth

Publisher's Cataloging-in-Publication Data
Names: Strand, Jennifer, author.
Title: Jacqueline Kennedy / by Jennifer Strand.
Description: Minneapolis, MN : Abdo Zoom, 2018. | Series: First ladies |
    Includes bibliographical references and index.
Identifiers: LCCN 2017931121 | ISBN 9781532120169 (lib. bdg.) |
    ISBN 9781614797272 (ebook) | 9781614797838 (Read-to-me ebook)
Subjects: LCSH: Onassis, Jacqueline Kennedy, 1929-1994--Juvenile literature. |
    Presidents spouses--United States--Biography--Juvenile literature. |
    Celebrities--United States--Biography--Juvenile literature.
Classification: DDC 973.922/092 [B]--dc23
LC record available at http://lccn.loc.gov/2017931121

Table of Contents

Introduction

Jacqueline Kennedy was a First Lady of the United States. Her husband was John F. Kennedy.

She made the White House
a center of **culture**.

Early Life

Jacqueline was born
on July 28, 1929.

She was called Jackie. In school Jackie was a hard worker. After college she worked for a newspaper.

Leader

Jackie married
John F. Kennedy in 1953.

He was a **lawmaker**. Jackie helped him with his **campaigns**.

The Kennedys traveled together. They spoke to crowds of people.

Many people
liked them.

In 1960 Jackie became the US First Lady.

She **redecorated** the White House.
She hosted fancy dinner parties.

Jackie supported the arts. She also traveled to several countries.

She introduced people around the world to American culture.

In 1963 President Kennedy
was killed. It was a sad time.

Jackie wanted people to remember her husband. She helped plan a library and museum.

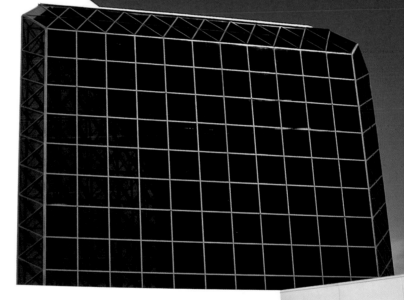

John F. Kennedy

PRESIDENTIAL LIBRARY AND MUSEUM

Later Jackie became an **editor**. She also remarried. On May 19, 1994, she died. She is remembered for celebrating American culture.

Quick Stats

Jacqueline Kennedy

Born: July 28, 1929

Birthplace: Southampton, New York

Husbands: John F. Kennedy (died), Aristotle Onassis

Years Served: 1961–1963

Known For: Jackie Kennedy was a US First Lady. She made American culture known around the world.

Died: May 19, 1994

Key Dates

1929: Jacqueline "Jackie" Lee Bouvier is born on July 28.

1953: She marries John F. Kennedy.

1961–1963: Jackie Kennedy is the First Lady. John F. Kennedy is the 35th US president.

1963: President Kennedy is killed on November 22.

1968: Jackie Kennedy marries Aristotle Onassis on October 20.

1994: Jackie Kennedy Onassis dies on May 19.

Glossary

campaign – the process of trying to get voted into office.

culture – the way of living in a place at a given time. Culture includes art, food, and customs.

editor – someone who works on text before it is published.

lawmaker – a person who makes laws.

redecorate – to change the look of a house by painting walls, getting new furniture, and more.

Booklinks

For more information on
Jacqueline Kennedy, please visit
abdobooklinks.com

Z⊙⊙m In on Biographies!

Learn even more with the Abdo Zoom
Biographies database. Check out
abdozoom.com for more information.

Index